MARIGOLD PRESS BOOKS
Your Story Matters

A division of International School of Story
Savannah, Georgia

www.marigoldpressbooks.org

All rights reserved. No part of this publication may be reproduced, stored in a retrieval system, or transmitted in any form or by any means, without the permission of the copyright holders.

Copyright ©2015 Emra Smith
Cover Design by Juan Espinosa
Interior Design by Rachael Hartman

Library of Congress Cataloging-in-Publication Data
Smith, Emra 1959
Your Story Matters

Library of Congress Control Number: 2015913855
ISBN: 978-1-942923-08-4 (paperback)

Bible versions used are noted within the text, and belong to the copyright holders thereof.

TeaTime Stories
The Essence of Why Your Story Matters

BY EMRA SMITH

Thank you Ollie,
You allowed Jesus to change your story
And therefore mine.
Thank You Jesus,
For leading each of us to have life through Your story.
Thank You that our stories matter to You.

Cease the busy.

Change the hurried cup of coffee
for a soothing cup of tea.

Get comfy.

Sink into a favorite chair.

Sip and be soul-stirred as never before.

Be still, and know that I am God.
Psalm 46:10 (ASV)

Be More. Live More. Love More.

God uniquely created you to
change the world in a way only you can.

Your Story Matters.
Each story matters.
The big stories.
The little stories.
Each one, every day.
Your entire life matters.
You matter.

Contents

Chapter 1 • My Big Story 11

Chapter 2 • A Little Story 21

Chapter 3 • Another Little Story 25

Chapter 4 • Your Story Matters 31

Chapter 5 • Who Are You? 35

Chapter 6 • What is Your Story? 45

Chapter 7 • Share Your Story 51

Chapter 8 • Every Story Has God In It 59

Chapter 9 • Will You Share Your Story? 63

Resources 70

With Deep Gratitude 72

Chapter 1
My Big Story

YOUR STORY MATTERS

Memories of my early childhood in South Africa elude me. I was barely a toddler when my tempestuous mother disappeared, leaving me with my gentle, loving father. Three years later she snatched me away to live in a new family with a stepdad. I felt confused. What happened to my sweet, kind daddy who loved me above all else? How does a little girl understand the complexities of the vast empty space in her heart?

She doesn't.

It would take years to recognize the repercussions of the deep longings for love unjustly denied in childhood, which were buried and tucked away. At the time, the hurts remained unrecognized, but gave my innocence an unkind fragility. I adjusted and learned to love my new family.

There were good times along with the transitions. I was barely nine years old when my family experienced a miracle. My stepdad was dying of a brain tumor and my mom, who was not a Christian, said to God, "If you heal this man, I promise You I will search for You all my life."

At that very moment my stepdad opened his eyes, awakening out of his coma. After a few months he came home and slowly learned to walk again. As a little girl I remember going to the doctors and seeing them shaking their heads, declaring his recovery an unexplained occurrence.

My mom kept her promise and searched for The Lord with all her heart and soul. We tested every form of Christianity you could imagine and eventually became Seventh-day Adventists. I believed in God with childlike faith, after seeing Him so clearly at work in the miracles of my stepdad's healing and my mother's conversion. All I wanted was to live for Jesus and to serve Him as a missionary. I gave my heart to Him in baptism when I was seventeen years old.

Four years later, I dropped out of college and leapt into marriage with all the joy, expectation and innocence of a young bride. I left my mother's home feeling all grown up and independent. My husband and I moved to a new city and started a business. Without realizing it, I tucked away the pain I felt from moving away from the life and people I knew and loved. I didn't allow myself to stop and reflect on how I felt about dropping out of college, deferring my dreams and pouring my heart into my husband's dreams. I believed together we would change the world for Jesus. My faith was strong and it carried me through the years ahead.

1 • My Big Story

We had just celebrated year one of marriage when our first daughter was born. Three years later we had a second daughter. Over the next six years, symptoms slowly unfolded and we learned our youngest had Cornelia De Lange Syndrome, which is a genetic disorder. It causes a range of physical, cognitive and medical challenges, which range from mild to severe. The news of my daughter's health made me feel as if I had fallen into a dark, black vortex. I became numb and quiet. I refused to feel my pain. Although my head knew what was happening, many years would pass before my heart felt the impact of her diagnosis.

I kept myself busy to cover up my pain, rather than address my hurts with The Lord and seek His healing. I chose to continue stepping boldly into each day, knowing God had a purpose in my daughter's disability. I did a great job of serving in the church, the community and my family. With a servant's heart I continued to give to everyone around me.

My soul was weighed down with physical exhaustion and a strong need to be seen, heard and tenderly loved. The dark void I fell into became a swirling pool, a loveless vacuum in need of laughter, lightness and fun. The empty hole, which began in childhood, yearned for tenderness, relief, and strength to uplift me. I didn't know how needy I was. I couldn't see it. I thought I was smart, strong and sophisticated, but I was weak and unaware. Over a period of eight years, I allowed spiritual emptiness to grow.

I became weary and vulnerable. I began to flirt with a comforter, which of course, had no place in a marriage. I fell into temptation and allowed my heart to attach to a man who was not my husband.

As the relationship grew I felt more and more miserable. Perhaps it was because I was breaking every spiritual truth and value I held dear. Or maybe it was because I believed the lie that I could find what I was missing in a man. I thought I could have all I longed for in the forbidden relationship.

I moved in and out of friendship with the man for over ten years. I kept turning away from God, rather than toward Him. Exhausted from an empty marriage, resisting my emotional affair, and raising a differently-abled daughter, my quiet desperate need for love grew.

I had a choice. I could seek God for His help, or I could reject Him and act in sin opting to take what was not mine to temporarily stop hurting. I foolishly chose the emotional affair and eventually it turned into a physical affair. I found myself further away from the freedom I longed for, freedom from the emotional pain of loss and loneliness.

During this time, my husband and I immigrated to the United States. Life spiraled on with fleeting moments of joy as I dived knee-deep into my first official job. Once again shrouded by loss and grief, the impact of assimilating to a new culture, and the monumental changes that took place, I was further depleted of my strength beyond my conscious awareness. Adding to my loss and stress, my mother died of sugar diabetes at the age of sixty-five. Aghast, I slipped into a dungeon of denial. I kept ignoring the warning signs of despair, weariness, and fragility. I never heard the silent cry for help, my soul shouted out for.

Life sped along and once more, I met another "wonderful man" who could fill my needs. I knew I didn't want to walk the adulterous path again. I finally ended my twenty-five year marriage. I was done. Done with my marriage; done with the struggle of moving toward and away from God. Done with everything. I wanted to be done with life and prayed God would send a truck, wipe me out and end it all. I plunged into grief and despair as darkness gripped my soul.

God waited patiently.

Have you ever noticed God allows us to come to the end of ourselves in order to bring us back to Him? Like the prodigal son, I had exhausted every avenue until the only thing left was to run to my heavenly Father. I was about to discover it was Him my soul longed for all along.

For the first time in my life I was alone. My girls were grown, the eldest married and the youngest living in a group home. It was just me. My old life was dead. Friends send flowers and cards to comfort those grieving the loss of a loved one to death. But with divorce there was no comfort, only a cold emptiness. I left my church and everything else I held dear. I sobbed myself to sleep each night, yet God pressed close, ever so gently. I vowed to be honest with myself and others, to see the state of my heart as it really was and to discover the hidden parts of my life. I went to see a psychologist and wrestled with learning how to love and care for myself. It was harder than I imagined. Still broken, I remarried a year after my divorce.

Yet God was so faithful and He drew me to Himself. Slowly, I began to heal. I became a Life Coach and had wonderful mentors, but without realizing it, humanism took hold of my thoughts. I began to believe I could do anything. I believed I could make a million dollars, and be who I wanted to be. The pendulum swung and I went from serving others to serving myself.

God waited patiently.

Six years later, my husband and I moved to sweet, sweet Savannah into a Christian community where I finally felt at home after the long years of loss. But only nine months later I faced another loss. My stepfather died of complications after falling and breaking his hip. He had outlived my mother by sixteen years. He was all I had left of my childhood. I went back to South Africa and felt my losses. On my return trip to Savannah, I cried out, "What is my purpose Lord?"

> "Share with everyone the incredibly, extravagant generosity of God."

In the sad, lonely weeks that followed, He answered my prayer and gave me what has become my personal mission statement: "Share with everyone the incredibly, extravagant generosity of God."

During the months ahead, He began to show me what He meant. As He healed me a little more each day, I began to see glimpses of His extravagant generosity in my own life.

I started to write a book, *Teatime Stories*, filled with the experiences of amazing women and what they achieved with inner strength, focus and willpower. An interesting transition happened as I started to write. God took my humanistic thinking and turned it upside down as I started to focus on Him as my source of life. The book needed to change focus as well. It had to be about God, how only He can go deep inside our souls and not just renew, but re-create us.

"Share your story; be vulnerable for Me."

God takes your story, which is composed of all you have experienced, wrapped in your personality, skills and the person you are, and molds you to become more than you could ever dream of. What a powerful, tender, compassionate, consistent and patient God He is. As you allow Him, He ultimately writes His story of love on your heart.

Today, God fills my soul, each crack and crevice. I am no longer drawn to try and fill the void of a father that was absent throughout my growing up years. No longer do I yearn or look for ways to satisfy my unmet needs.

God is enough. He is more than enough. All I yearn for now is more of Him. To know Him more and to pour my life into serving Him, however He asks.

And He does ask.

"Share your story; be vulnerable for Me."

But how could I? How could I bare my soul's shame and sadness? Then He showed me a picture of Himself on the cross, naked, at His most vulnerable, for all to see. Humiliated and overwhelmed with the ugliness of the world, even though He was King over it all. How horrific, and yet terribly beautiful.

My heart broke kneeling at the cross, and in its breaking God removed my shame. Somehow, sharing my story is so little compared to what He did and does for me.

I am no longer the woman I once was. Because of Jesus I am more. I love more and I am learning to live more in His purpose for me. And it's all because of Him. All I see is Him.

He is incredible and extravagant and generous, above measure!

> *"For this, O LORD, I will praise you among the nations;*
> *I will sing praises to Your name."*
> Psalm 18:49 (NLT)

Chapter 2

A Little Story

Where lessons are learned

YOUR STORY MATTERS

We all have a big story to share. Our big stories reveal the direction of our lives and all the things that inherently make up who we are: our personalities, skills, beliefs, fears, longings and experiences. But life is filled with our little stories as well. The everyday happenings that slip by almost unnoticed. Sometimes we think our little stories don't matter, but ultimately it is the accumulation of our little stories that form our big story.

Sometimes, in the ordinary and busy crushing of everyday life, we lose sight of our little stories and miss their importance. I've found it helpful to journal and capture the impact of my little stories, to keep them from slipping away and losing their impact. Our lives are lived in ordinary, small-story moments. The small stories are where we see the beauty, richness and depth of life. It is here we are molded and prepared for the big things.

Our lives are lived in ordinary, small-story moments.

Not long ago, I wrote the following entry in my journal.

April 2, 2015

Once again it seems as if a myriad of decisions lie before me. Transition seems imminent again, and with changes comes the question, "What do I really want to do with my life?"

Do I want to work the day-in and day-out grind for someone else, or continue to climb the peaks and valleys of growing my own business?

Should we move near the kids, stay where we are or choose a place my heart desires? It's crazy living in a country with so many options, and each one could work.

How do I balance my commitment to everyone I love, my family, community and friends, with my passion for serving others?

Does money impact my decisions? Should it?

Tired. Too many thoughts. Head is swirling. Time out is needed. Quit thinking. Be still my soul. I'm here, Lord . . . I need time with You.

. . .

Reflecting on this journal entry I realized that I learned a lot. I had taken a time out, and sat under the shade of a huge tree beside two pools of water. One pool was hot, the other cold. It was the perfect place to write and then submerge myself into the water to reflect and listen.

The experience of taking time to spend with God, to be still and listen, was like immersing into the hot pool of water, allowing the heat to wrap around me and relax each tired muscle. At some point in the process, I knew it was time to step out of the hot water, to jump into a cold pool, let go of the heat, and absorb the cold. Then step back into the hot water where the warmth impacted my body anew and the experience ignited again.

My hot- and cold-pool experience parallels my time with God. In His presence is all I long for: peace, deep joy, rest, removal of pain, and rejuvenation. Spending time with God is like sitting in the hot water.

But if I just sit soaking, receiving, eventually the water's effect dissipates. I need to get up, trade the wonder of the heat for a cold place, and then in the right time return back to the heat. Jumping in a cold pool prepares me for the hot water to relax my body again.

The hot water—God's presence—is where I receive from God. Moving to the cold water is like the experience of giving to others what I have received from Him.

We must return to Him again to be replenished anew. Be immersed. Go give. Be immersed. Go give. Always going back and forth.

> **I invite you now to take another sip of tea.**
> **Pause. Ponder.**
> **Join me in a time of rest with Jesus.**
> **Leave all the questions of your life behind.**
> **Enter into the hot water, as it were.**
> **Be open to listen.**
> **See Him.**
> **Hear Him and what He has for you.**
> **Write down the thoughts you hear from Him.**

Chapter 3

Another Little Story

A Conversation Between Jesus and Me

Jesus, You experienced everything that's ugly here on earth so that I can know beauty unimaginable. A beauty that is found in Your story. For You, too, have a big story . . .

> **The story of eternity.**
> **The story of earth.**
> **The story of conquering death.**
> **Your story of relentless love.**

You have little stories as well, made of your constant interactions with us. You see the sparrow fall. You see my broken heart. You count my tears. You hear me sigh in weariness. You know when my spirit is crushed. You understand and call when I hide from life and run from You.

When compared against eternity and creation, these little stories seem so insignificant. Yet they matter to You. You care. We matter to You. Our stories matter because Your stories matter. You long to write Your story through our lives.

We hunger for more but our hunger gets twisted, the focus shifts and we develop a thirst that cannot be satisfied. We scribble our little stories of the things we yearn for: tender love, passion, money, clothes, gorgeous homes, entertainment, and fame. Why do we run after these desires that only bring moments of pleasure—inanimate, yes, lifeless moments? Why do we keep chasing dead objects, slamming into brick walls? We are left with nothing, nada, zilch. Empty.

How silly and small-minded we are. Quenching our thirst is exactly what Your life in us is all about. Despite it all, You want to write Your story in us.

Jesus, help me keep my focus on You. I want to remember, in each minute of every day, that You are hungry to communicate, guide, and teach me. You want to show me the sweetness each decision with You can bring. You anxiously wait to share Your wisdom with me. You have intimate knowledge of me. You made me. You know each solution that I am so blind to. What keeps me from leaning into You alone? Why seek anything from anyone, or anywhere else, but You? I know from experience that You alone are the One that satisfies my deepest longing for love.

"The sinful choices you make break My heart because I know they'll hurt you. Sometimes, it's the little things you ignore that do the most damage.

3 • Another Little Story

"Remember when your weariness closed about you? Feeling alone and exasperated, your heart needed tender love.

"I'd call you to unburden your pain to Me. Sometimes you did, sometimes you didn't. You tried harder in your marriage, gave it all you had and when you'd run into dead ends, emptiness consumed you and you'd become discouraged. You shut me out and eventually you became captivated by an outsider.

"I called, I whispered, sometimes shouted. Your Bible became dusty, you traded your time in prayer, sacrificed it on the altar of busyness. You couldn't hear Me. Blindness crept in and feelings took over.

"Sin is simply separation from Me, followed by acts with consequences. If I'm not the focus, something else is, and then it becomes your god. Sin always hurts you and often results in you hurting others. Then my heart breaks when you hurt."

But Jesus, You conquered sin, I do not have to be bound by it. The battle is not endless. I have seen the incredible change in my life. Yet, You keep uncovering different areas in my life that need growth and change. Smart money management for one, consistently guarding my diet and exercise another! I know your power is there for me to rise above these things, yet it's as if my head knows, but my heart does not. The neural pathways, my habits, will need to change.

"That's easy. Follow Me. Copy what I did. It's in the Book. Read it daily. By beholding Me, you become changed. Yes, my love, I Am the Way, the Truth and the Life. (John 14:6 NIV)

"All those the Father gives me will come to Me, and whoever comes to Me I will never drive away. (John 6:37 NIV)

"Come to Me. Abide in Me. If you abide in Me, I will abide in you. If I am in you, you will receive all power, life to the full, peace that surpasses all understanding." (Matthew 11:28; John 15:4; Acts 1:8; John 10:10; Philippians 4:7)

You are truly love. Absolute and complete. So patient and kind. You're all that matters.

"And You matter to me. I love you my child. I gave My all for you. Find freedom in My love. There's life in My love, in Me.

"I am Life. Love Me. Have life. Please. I love you."

My heart is now quiet. Still. Resting. Thinking . . .

Chapter 4

Your Story Matters

Our conversation continues

Without You, Lord, our stories are meaningless. Some are good; some are sad. A few will be remembered, most won't. A few of us will achieve our dreams, but the majority never will. Life is short. It ends. It's over. We're left with nothing.

But, with You, life is now and forever. Life now is filled with challenges. Life forever is perfect. I can hardly dream of it. With you, death's impact is lessened.

"While you're on Earth, when you live for Me you get a taste, a glimpse of forever. Let's adventure together. I'm with you all the way. See everything, yes, everything, through My eyes. Can you imagine the journey? I promise, if I fully enter your story, You will love each day, whether or not the sun is shining.

> I am the God of abundance.
> I am the God of creation.
> I am the God of more.
> I am the God of beauty.
> I am the God of laughter.
> I am the God of rescue.

**I am the God of support.
I am the God of re-creating.
I am the God of love.**

"I love you. You are loved. I died for You. I created You. I am re-creating You. Your story matters to Me because you matter to Me."

Love, Jesus

• • •

Do you understand your story matters because you matter to Him? If we did not matter to God, The Ruler and Creator of all and Giver of eternal life, would our stories matter in an eternal context? Would they hold the same power, impact and meaning?

I think not.

Imagine if there were no eternal implications to our stories. If that were so, and if our earth blew up today and became a pile of ash, all of our great stories would be gone as if they never were.

Yet, if there is life with Him after this life, our stories matter. Our stories matter to God because we matter to Him. The perfect, powerful God of the universe became one of us to give us the gift of life with Him forever. Our stories are about Him. Our

Our stories matter to God because we matter to Him.

stories show His love, teach how to live, and embody peace and an incomprehensible joy.

In the next few chapters we are going to look at the God-meaning of our story. How did He weave you together? What is His intentional design for you? How can you ignite your passion into His purpose, and meet the needs of others on His behalf? How does His story play out through your life?

If you don't fully grasp why you matter to God, or why your story is important, refer to the resources listed in the back of this book.

> **Your story matters.**
> **You are your story.**
> **You matter.**
> **Because of Jesus.**

Chapter 5

Who Are You?

YOUR STORY MATTERS

> Do you know how you function?
> What are your strengths?
> Weaknesses?
> Core values?
> Needs?
> Spiritual gifts?
> Limiting beliefs?
> Fears?

Knowing how you're created and pieced together facilitates wise decision-making both for you and others around you.

When we decided to move to Savannah, a city we barely knew existed, I was beyond excited about the new adventure. Yet during the first few months we lived here, my heart and soul experienced torment. Anxiety, loneliness and a deep sadness wove between the joy and delight of new discoveries. I was confused at my contrary emotions, yet I came to understand them after becoming a DISC Facilitator.

DISC is a behavioral analysis tool. As a facilitator, I guide people to understand why they do what they do. As

I applied DISC to my own life, I discovered I am an "I." It means I'm an influencer, outgoing, ready for fun and change. I am also an "S," meaning consistent, choosing stability. I'll readily accept change, even jump into it, but when the quiet sets in, the ease and comfort will dissipate and stress will come knocking.

I've learned skills to manage my varied emotional responses, and my emotions no longer take over my experience of life every time I face conflict. My primary go-to place is God's Word, prayer, quiet solitude, rest and waiting. Yes, I'm learning patience through it all.

Looking back at the little stories within my big stories, I cannot help but see how my lack of not understanding my fears, needs and core values impacted my behavior. I did not realize I had fear of conflict, or that one of my core values was joy and fun. The way I'd deal with conflict was to avoid it or acquiesce, put it aside, and create the smiling, laughing, happy moments elsewhere.

For example, when my girls were young, many afternoons I chose to take my eldest daughter for tea and shopping instead of going home to face yet another upheaval with my disabled daughter. I knew the evening and night would be filled with her sleeplessness and that the next day I would bravely step into it all again.

What could I have done differently had I better known myself?

I would have faced conflict, learned to accept that my second daughter had challenges, and I would have found help. I would find a support group and Mommies' groups where all the children had complexities; a place where there'd be more understanding and sharing. Yes, I would still take Big Sister for tea and shopping alone, but my underlying, unresolved layer of despair would have been manageable.

As a young wife, I tried force my need to make a difference into my first husband's priorities for his life. I was trying to live through him, but that was not sustainable. I started exploring my gifts and living more within my strengths. As I changed, my relationship with my ex-husband changed. He was not accustomed to me living for God. Conflict increased between us, and I tried to avoid it finding fun other places. The way I was behaving wasn't fair to either me or to my ex-husband. Sadly, the marriage ended.

With all I've learned, the stories within my marriage now are different than they were in my first marriage. Now I am so much more of who God created me to be and my marriage is laced with mutual respect and understanding. In learning about myself, I realized I have a strong need to make a difference using my God-given gifts.

With God's help and deeper wisdom in our marriage today, my husband and I respect each other's strengths. I began to live out God's calling on my life, and I no longer expect my husband to live it out for, or even with, me. What a difference it has made in daily life.

Knowing ourselves facilitates wiser choices and decisions for today and days yet to follow. We are born into this world living for ourselves. Just watch babies; they are all about their needs from their first cry. But so often we grow up unaware of our true selves and needs. The people, experiences and stories of life often shut us down. The hurt, pain and indulgences we experience dull our hearts to those around us.

We all must learn that Jesus is The Essence of Life. Perhaps we once knew it was all about Him, but somewhere in our life's journey we have forgotten or ignored the Truth, or maybe we never heard it before.

Jesus was clear as to what life is all about:

> *"Jesus replied: 'Love the Lord your God with all your heart and with all your soul and with all your mind. This is the first and greatest commandment. And the second is like it: Love your neighbor as yourself. All the Law and the prophets hang on these two commandments."*
> Matthew 22:38-40 (NIV)

. . .

Love God.
Love others.
Love who He made you to be.

5 • Who Are You?

Do you love God?
Do you love others?
Do you love yourself?

Matthew 22 tells us we are to first love God, and then to love others as we love ourselves. It took me what will probably be more than half of my life to realize I cannot have a healthy love for others if I do not know God, allow Him to heal my known and unknown maladies and to create in me a healthy self-love.

Like me, you cannot properly love others without first seeing yourself as God sees you and accepting and loving yourself. You must come to know God, and allow Him to show you how wonderfully and purposefully you are made. It's in the process of knowing you are God's created one where you learn what love, care and respect is.

There is a difference between self-obsession and loving yourself with God's love. Being self-obsessed, or ego-centric, reflects as pride, arrogance and greed. It's shallow and plastic. When you are obsessed with yourself, your love for others will change depending on what most benefits you. A self-obsessed love is never about the other person, your neighbor, but always about you. The heart of one who is self-obsessed is a vacuum of need impossible to fill, as mine was. It is a place where peace eludes and a thirst and hunger for "more" perpetuates. It is a space that devours everything, and spirals into a black vortex. It's a horrid place to be.

When you learn to love through God's eyes you enter a place of strength and wise decision-making. You grow in wisdom and live in peace. Your life is centered as you sit at Jesus' feet and learn about Him. In turn, He empowers you to positively impact other people. As you learn to love yourself with God's love, His love creates room to love and care for others. When God fills you with His own love, you have plenty of love to give without depletion.

> **As you learn to love yourself with God's love, His love creates room to love and care for others.**

When you are filled with God's love, you become the pool of hot water for your neighbor and loved one. You become the place they jump into from their cold pool. You facilitate the warm embrace of healing and relaxation. You become Jesus' love for them. You give from the strength you find in Him. Love is Jesus gift to us. His words of life make for wise-living. He knows how life works. He made us and leaves no mystery about maximized living.

> *"For You created my inmost being;*
> *You knit me together in my mother's womb.*
> *I praise you because I am fearfully and wonderfully made;*
> *Your works are wonderful, I know that full well."*
> Psalm 139:13.14 (NIV)

You are fearfully and wonderfully made. Do you know that full well? I want to ask again, who did God make you to be? Who are you? What is His purpose for your life?

Who will you love with Jesus' love today? When you know the answer to the questions, you begin to understand why you act the way you do.

As you embrace God's love, you begin to love who He has made you to be, who He is currently making you to become, and ALL He created within you. You clearly see why you make decisions the way you do. You see what's present and what's missing in your life.

If you want to discover more about how God wove you together, refer to the resources in the back of this book.

Your new vision enables you to see God in your life and your need for Him. It compels you to find renewal, strength, clarity and peace in Him. As you journey in close encounter with God, you can shout and sing as David did in this Psalm . . .

> *"Wonderful are Your works, and my soul knows it very well."*
> Psalm 139:14 (NASB)

Understanding what you're comprised of helps you understand missteps of the past and allows you to extend to yourself the graciousness Christ gives you so freely. Once you accept God's forgiveness, and learn to forgive yourself, you are equipped to forgive others. Forgiving others is essential in your walk with the Lord. Showing grace toward yourself, forgiving yourself for hurt and pain you've caused and experienced, and letting go of

As you experience abundant life in Christ, you begin to open the door of forgiveness toward others.

any resentment you may harbor is a complex task—only possible through God's power. As you experience abundant life in Christ, you begin to open the door of forgiveness toward others.

Accept Christ's forgiveness.
Forgive yourself.
Forgive others.

"I, even I, am the One who takes away your sins because of Who I am. And I will not remember your sins. Make Me remember, and let us talk together. Make your cause known, that you may be shown not to be guilty."
Isaiah 43:25, 26 (NLV)

"When you stand to pray, if you have anything against anyone, forgive him. Then your Father in heaven will forgive your sins also."
Mark 11:25 (NLV)

Stand in front of the mirror. Look at yourself. Do you see a beautiful work in process?

You are fearfully and wonderfully designed, created, and shaped. You are perfect in Him. Accept the gift of forgiveness. Know what Jesus did for you at the cross. He paid the price for sin in your place. See Christ in the mirror, reflected in you as His creation. He gave all He has for you. When God looks at you, He sees perfect. Yes, you, perfect. Yes, you're in the process of becoming like Him, and it's a perfect process. Remember:

> *"The faithful love of the Lord never ends!*
> *... His mercies begin afresh each morning."*
> Lamentations 3:22-23 (NLT)

You are His. You are loved. You are beautiful.

Chapter 6
What is Your Story?

Once you know and accept that you are beautiful and loved, you begin to look at your big story and each of the little stories in it through a different lens. You begin to see the things through God's eyes. You can step into you stories with Jesus, hear Him speak, allow Him to heal and make sense of it all.

> As you look over your life with Jesus,
> He unfolds your stories,
> Unwraps all you've hidden away,
> Unties what holds you back,
> Discards the unnecessary,
> Keeps the treasure, and
> Remodels what is left.

**If you allow God the honor,
He will gently unlock your heart—story by story.**

*"If you need wisdom, ask our generous God,
and He will give it to you. He will not rebuke you for asking."*
James 1:5 (NLT)

Make a list of each of your stories that come to mind. Later, go back and fill-in the details of each story—big and small. Ponder on each person and scenario that comes to mind, note your emotions, and ask God to make sense of it. Take responsibility for your part in the issue and apologize when it's beneficial. Ask Jesus to forgive you for harboring anger, bitterness, guilt or fear—none of which are from God. Let go of your pain.

> *"This is how I want you to conduct yourself in these matters. If you enter your place of worship and, about to make an offering, you suddenly remember a grudge a friend has against you, abandon your offering, leave immediately, go to this friend and make things right. Then and only then, come back and work things out with God."*
> Matthew 5:23-24 (MSG)

As you work through your story with God in prayer and contemplation, enter into a place of worship. Offer your life and stories to God. Allow Him to cleanup and bring order to your chaos.

Giving your stories to God is not about reconciling relationships; that is God's job. Your job is to let go, take responsibility to repent for holding grudges, harboring anger and justifying your emotions. As you follow God's lead, make amends. It doesn't matter how the other person responds. Simply obey what God tells you to do, and let go.

Giving your stories to God is not about reconciling relationships; that is God's job.

There are times you may need help in processing your story. Find a trusted friend, pastor or mentor who will listen to you, offer godly counsel and pray with you. Perhaps you need professional help or a Christian life coach. Listen to The Holy Spirit's prompting and heed it. He wants the junk out. He wants to free you from the negative impact of the past you hold onto.

• • •

What's next? Thank God for removing the negativity! No matter how you feel, believe it's gone! Accept the truth—the past is over!

Allow Almighty God to step in and heal you, to enable you to forgive, to forget and move on. Remember He is God, the Living God. The One who changes you, who elevates your life, and expands your reach.

> *"Once again You will show loving concern for us.*
> *You will completely wipe out the evil things we've done.*
> *You will throw all our sins into the bottom of the sea."*
> Micah 7:19 (NIRV)

As He pulls the weeds out of your life, He creates space to grow the beauty He is planting inside—His beauty. We are made in His image.

> *"So God created mankind in his own image,*
> *in the image of God He created them;*

male and female He created them."
Genesis 1:27 (NIV)

You belong to God and He is re-creating His beautiful image in you. He is the true Life-giver!

*"We are God's masterpiece.
He has created us anew in Christ Jesus
so we can do the good things He planned for us long ago."*
Ephesians 2:10 (NLT)

You are beautiful.
You are unique.
Your Story Matters.

Chapter 7
Share Your Story

Stories breathe life, hope and courage to others.

Mindful sharing your story during a dark time can be part of your healing process. As you share, sometimes you are the encourager, and other times you may need encouragement. Needing encouragement is normal; clouds surround and descend upon us all. Allowing another person to help lift the load relieves the strain from your heart. It becomes a promise of light in the dark.

You may have many questions as you begin to share your story. Who do you share with? Do you share randomly with strangers without emotional restraint? When do you share? Where is your safe place to share?

During your moments of questioning, drop to your knees. Pour out your questions to Jesus. Give your doubts and fears to The One who said:

"Are you tired? Worn out? Burned out on religion?
Come to Me. Get away with Me and you'll recover your life.
I'll show you how to take a real rest.
Walk with Me and work with Me—watch how I do it.

> *Learn the unforced rhythms of grace.*
> *I won't lay anything heavy or ill-fitting on you.*
> *Keep company with Me and*
> *you'll learn to live freely and lightly."*
> Matthew 11:28-30 (MSG)

As you seek wisdom and lean into the Lord He will tell you when to share and for what purpose. Sometimes you will journey alone with God to resolve your burden. At times you may share with a wise counselor or a trusted friend who knows how to listen and pray as you and God work through your story.

Whatever you dwell on will pour out of you.

Dig into The Word; spend hours, days and weeks in prayer. Do whatever it takes to heal. Listen. Be still. Wait expectantly. Believe your heart will heal, and that you will gain wisdom. God is with you, as He promised.

> *"You're My servant, serving on My side.*
> *I've picked you. I haven't dropped you.*
> *Don't panic. I'm with you.*
> *There's no need to fear for I'm your God.*
> *I'll give you strength. I'll help you.*
> *I'll hold you steady, keep a firm grip on you."*
> Isaiah 41:9-10 (MSG)

Your cloudy moments and times of darkness become your strength and voice when it's your time to be a shoulder to lean on or an ear to listen. One day, you will become the encourager. You will be His hands to touch, His arms to embrace, His voice to speak, His ears to listen.

> *"Share each other's troubles and problems,*
> *and so obey our Lord's command."*
> Galatians 6:2 (TLB)

I must insert a self-check here. Are you allowing Christ's life-giving healing touch to root out the past holding you back from your full potential? You must measure to see if you are growing spiritually. Use the following simple gauge:

> *"A good man produces good deeds from a good heart.*
> *And an evil man produces evil deeds*
> *from his hidden wickedness.*
> *Whatever is in the heart overflows into speech."*
> Luke 6:45 (TLB)

Whatever you dwell on will pour out of you. Take inventory of your words, behavior, body language and attitude. You must not try to hide what goes on in your heart—not from God, or from yourself. In your moments of realization (and realize them you must), if you are to love your neighbor as yourself, you must first step back into God's embrace. You must allow Him to wash you with His love and forgiveness. You must allow Him to change you. It's a simple process. He makes it easy because He

You do not have to become perfect before you can share Jesus with others.

does the work. Soak in His warm water, and you'll be ready to face the cold world.

"It is absolutely clear that God has called you to a free life.
Just make sure that you don't use this freedom as an excuse
to do whatever you want to do and destroy your freedom.
Rather, use your freedom to serve one another in love;
that's how freedom grows. For everything we know about
God's Word is summed up in a single sentence:
Love others as you love yourself.
That's an act of true freedom.
If you bite and ravage each other, watch out—in no time at all
you will be annihilating each other,
and where will your precious freedom be then?"
Galatians 5:13, 15 (MSG)

Love one another.
Be mindful and careful.
You spirit will soar when you unburden with care.

Note the threads of how God unpacks your stories. Ultimately it rids you of hurtful emotions and prevents you from passing them on to other people. The process is marvelous:

The unpacking.
The healing.
The re-shaping.
The growing.
You explode with joy and health.
It cannot be contained.

7 • Share Your Story

He is changing you.
He has changed you.
You live the exuberant life,
Even in your dark, cloudy moments
Your perspective is different.

Look who He has made you to be:
AMAZING,
INCREDIBLE,
BEAUTIFUL,
EMPOWERED,
HIS . . .

*"Jesus said, 'Go home to your own people.
Tell them your story—what the Master did, how he had mercy
on you.' The man went back and began to preach in the Ten
Towns area about what Jesus had done for him.
He was the talk of the town."*
Mark 5:18-20 (MSG)

Tired after a day of speaking to the crowds, Jesus and his core leaders left on a boat and crossed to the other side of the sea. The minute they stepped out of the boat a frantic, wild, enraged man ran toward them. Jesus healed him. It was a miracle. You can read the amazing details in the book of Mark in the Bible. When Jesus left, the man wanted to go with Him. Wouldn't you? But Jesus told him to go home and tell everyone what He had done for him. You see Jesus Himself did not stay and work in those ten towns, yet the people needed healing and hope and life. Jesus needed a man to do the work on behalf of Him. He chose the once wild man of the Gerasene. The man answered the call.

> *"And he went away and began to proclaim in the Decapolis how much Jesus had done for him, and everyone was amazed."*
> Mark 5:20 (NRSV)

The man became Jesus' hands and feet, ears, eyes and mouth. He changed the world he lived in. He brought life, hope, healing and joy through the Name of Jesus. You do not have to become perfect before you can share Jesus with others. The man didn't spend years following Jesus before sharing his story. Jesus told him to share what happened to him that very same day. If we allow Jesus to be our Savior, we are qualified to tell others what He has done for us. Will there be more to learn? Yes. Can you change your world by simply sharing your story? Yes. Your personal story of Jesus is stronger than a well-planned and researched sermon from the smartest theologian or famous preacher.

> *"O give thanks to the Lord,*
> *call on His name,*
> *make known His deeds among the peoples.*
> *Sing to Him, sing praises to Him:*
> *Tell of His wonderful works."*
> Psalm 105:1 (NRSV)

Others will come to know Jesus if you share Him. How can you not share? How can you hold back His love and life from anyone you love?

> *"When you produce much fruit,*
> *you are my true disciples.*
> *This brings great glory to my Father."*
> John 15:8 (NLT)

Chapter 8

Every Story Has God In It

Do you see Him in your story?

On your darkest days, when the sun doesn't shine, in order to see God you will need to shift your perspective. He is there in your difficulties and will use your dark stories if you allow Him to. He promised to see you through. You'll learn new things about yourself, about life, and about Him. You'll be able to give strength, courage and hope to someone else when you're through the storm.

Changing your perspective, your thoughts, is a powerful experience. Looking through God's lens enables you to step into His power so that your situation no longer controls you. Note what happens:

> *"For God did not give us a spirit of timidity*
> *(of cowardice, of craven and cringing and fawning fear),*
> *but [He has given us a spirit] of power and of love and of*
> *calm and well-balanced mind and discipline and self-control."*
> 2 Timothy 1:7 (AMP)

> *"But do not conform any longer to the pattern of this world,*
> *but be transformed by the renewing of your mind.*
> *Then you will be able to test and approve what God's will is –*

> *His good, pleasing and perfect will."*
> Romans 12:2 (NIV)

> *"We demolish arguments and every pretention that sets itself up against the knowledge of God, and we take captive every thought to make it obedient to Christ."*
> 2 Corinthians 10:5 (NIV)

> *"For as he thinks in his heart, so is he."*
> Proverbs 23:7 (NKJV)

Spend time meditating on God's Word, talk to Him, journal as you move through your storm. Listen. Look for His transforming power in your story and then be ready to share.

Is every story sharable? No not all the time, and not every time. At times the environment is not ready. The other person isn't ready to listen. We may not be ready or healed enough to share our story. Perhaps the time is not right.

It is important not to share stories of woe for the sake of misery, or to stay in pain. We share our stories to heal, uplift, embrace, encourage, and to be encouraged. But do be careful to not hide in the comfort of your discomfort to merely stay safe. Jesus didn't stay in His safe place. He left His safety to save you and me. Stay in tune with The Holy Spirit and listen to His promptings. He will direct you.

8 • Every Story Has God In It

> *"The sheep that are My own hear*
> *And are listening to My voice;*
> *and I know them, and they follow Me."*
> John 10:27 (AMP)

> *"And your ears will hear a word behind you, saying,*
> *This is the way; walk in it, when you turn to the right hand*
> *and when you turn to the left."*
> Isaiah 30:21 (AMP)

Abide in Him. Draw close to God through prayer and time in The Word—and lots of it.

> *"For I know the plans I have for you, says the Lord.*
> *They are plans for good and not for evil,*
> *to give you a future and a hope."*
> Jeremiah 29:11 (TLB)

> *"It is clear to us, friends,*
> *that God not only loves you very much*
> *but also has put His hand on you*
> *for something special."*
> 1 Thessalonians 1:4 (MSG)

How can you not go and tell what He has done for you? Your story Matters. You Matter. Tell His life-giving story through yours. He Matters.

Chapter 9
Will You Share Your Story?

*"Go back home and tell everyone
how much God has done for you."*
Luke 8:39 (CEV)

*"But Jesus came and spoke these words to them,
'All power in Heaven and on earth has been given to Me.
You, then, are to go and make disciples of all the nations
and baptize them in the name of the Father
and of the Son and of the Holy Spirit.
Teach them to observe all that I have commanded you and,
remember, I am with you always,
even to the end of the world.'"*
Matthew 28:18-20 (PHILLIPS)

God has healed my heart, peeled back layer after layer during this life-changing process, and enabled me to see the gifts He has given me through each of my stories. God walked with me through professional counseling after my divorce. He brought astounding Life Coaches and mentors into my life. Each person has helped me discover more of how God put me together and what He designed me for.

God empowers me to live out my mission statement: *"Sharing with everyone I meet the incredible extravagant generosity of God"* (Acts 20:24 MSG). My purpose is clear: facilitate the process for women to discover the beauty of their story, and then step into His story through theirs.

I offer coaching, speaking, teaching, writing and retreats to help women discover God's beauty and healing. I empower women to step into their story and share through speaking, podcasts and writing on my blog and *Teatime Stories* books. *Teatime Stories* began with my story and testimony of the power of what God does with the details of our lives.

Let me share a small story of what God has done in my life through *Teatime Stories*. Believe me, I am smiling ear to ear at the wonder of God's generous extravagance and excellence in providing comfort for my heart.

Let's take our final sip of tea together for today as I share.

Tea has always been a part of my life and teatime one of the few sweet moments I shared with my mom. Having tea became my treasured way to spend precious moments with my girlfriends and eldest daughter. Hosting tea parties and selling tea has recently also become an answer to prayer, and a fun, product-based business, which compliments my ministry. When sharing about this opportunity with my youngest daughter, I never imagined that she would want to become part of it. With gusto she asked to do it too. What a gift to my disabled daughter's life! To see her joy and pride in it reminds me that there are no limits in life with God.

Tea is my go-to beverage at home to soothe my soul and palette. Now Jesus uses it for Him in a myriad of ways! Why would He not, if it's a treasured experience to connect me to others and others to Him? God met me in a warm heart-place and embraced me there, soothing my soul like a warm cup of tea. I did not choose my ministries and business; I'm not smart enough to put it all together. But He is. Slowly He has brought it all together, piece by piece, one assignment and then the next and the next.

He has taken ALL He has given me and is rolling it into the desires and needs of my heart. I have fun hosting tea parties. I experience deep joy at providing a space for women to share their stories. My gifts all work together and facilitate my desire to be a missionary and share Jesus. It is so sweet to stick close to the Lord and see Him bring completeness in so many ways.

"Now to Him who is able to do more
abundantly above all that we ask or think.
According to the power that works within us.
To Him be the glory in the church and in Christ Jesus
To all generations forever and ever."
Ephesians 3:21 (NASB)

**Are you ready to allow God to stir and fill
your soul with all He has for you?**

Here is how I can help facilitate your discovery and empower you to share His story through yours.

Discovery and Stepping into Story:
- New Life Story Group® Coaching
- 1:1 Coaching
- Identity & Destiny: 7 Steps to Discovering God's will for your life
- His Story Through You Retreats
- Communication Skills Workshops

Encouragement, Motivation, Teaching:
- Teatime Stories books
- Your Story Matters book
- Blogging
- Speaking

Platform to Share His Story Through Yours:
- *Teatime Stories books.* Soul stirring stories of women; when Christ intersected their story and what happened next.

- *Teatime Stories Chapter Teas* (small groups). Regular gatherings of women who share a cup of tea and sweet stories of Christ's power with their neighbors who may not have the privilege to hear so outside of a tea party.

- *Teatime Stories Chapter Leaders* (leadership development). Become a leader. You can facilitate teas with women, thus responding to the simple call of Jesus "to go and tell."

- *Write and speak your story.* Allow me to share your story, post to blog, publish in a book, and interview you on my podcast.

EmraSmith.com

Resources

Scriptures On Our Great God

Psalm 8: 3-4 — God is creative and powerful.

Psalm 95:3 — God is above all gods.

Psalm 136:12 — God's mercy endures forever.

Psalm 147:5 — God is mighty.

Isaiah 26:4 — God is everlasting strength.

Isaiah 40:28 — God never gets weary.

Isaiah 55:8,9 — God's ways are higher than ours.

Jeremiah 10:12 — God created the earth with His power, wisdom and discretion.

Zephaniah 3:17 — God is mighty, saves, rejoices and loves you.

Luke 12:7 — God knows your worth.

John 3:16 — God gave His Son to save us.

Romans 5:8 — God loves us and proved it.

Romans 8:1-4 — God does not condemn us; He frees us through Jesus' blood.

Romans 8:28 — God uses all things for His purpose.

2 Corinthians 5:17 — God makes us new in Jesus.

2 Corinthians 13:4 — God gives us power for life.

There are many more scriptures that reveal who God is and how He loves you. I pray you dig into God's Word and find joy and strength as you discover new scriptures about who God is, and who you are in Christ.

Recommended Reading

Epic: The Story God is Telling, by John Eldredge

Restless, by Jennie Allen

100 Days of Right Believing, by Joseph Prince

He Made Me Resources

Identity & Destiny: 7 Steps to a Purpose-filled Life, by Tom and Pam Wolf

Perfectly You Program, by Dr. Caroline Leaf

Strengthsfinder, www.gallupstrengthscenter.com

Live a New Life Story, by David Krueger
(Group and 1:1 Coaching)

With Deep Gratitude

Being vulnerable and giving my story to God is changing me in ways so vast, the awe of the process fills me with wonder. Every day God unravels more within my life stories. He heals, expands and puts them to use in a myriad of ways. Wow! Humble. Excited. Thankful.

My gratitude and wonder of God knows no end. Thank you Father. Thank you Jesus. Every day I sing a new song of thanks to You.

I have a heart of warmth, love and thanks for Kathy Burnsed, Bucky Burnsed and Laura Fulford who have labored over my writing, the words and thoughts in this book. Thank you for your time, care, directness and love of Jesus to ensure that He is represented correctly.

Thank you Rachael Hartman. What a publisher! You have made this easier, given me peace and confidence in the process. I treasure you.

Thank you Karen Pearson for pouring your gifts into my life, my writing and this book. Thank you for sharing our God-journey together. I love and adore you.

I am deeply grateful for the mentors that have contributed in such meaningful ways to my life: Gary Rust, Juanita Kretschmar, Dr. Dave Krueger, Pam & Tom Wolf, Jo Crosby and Ingrid VanderVeldt. Your gifts, wisdom and stories invested in me has been multiplied, as I now in turn share with others.

Thank you to my family, Lianro, Anthony, Levi, Sage, Candice and Roberdy. You impact my life every day with your love, life-lessons and laughter.

Emra Smith

A division of International School of Story
Savannah, Georgia

www.marigoldpressbooks.org

www.ingramcontent.com/pod-product-compliance
Lightning Source LLC
Chambersburg PA
CBHW070104120526
44588CB00034B/2240